LEADING TECHNOLOGY FOR MULTIPLE NEXT-LEVELS SYSTEMS EVOLUTION

Integrating systems, departments, people, and processes for new competitive advantage

Brian Iinuma and Eric Klauss

Published by Strategic Systems Group, Inc.

ISBN 978-0-9993096-1-2

Disclaimer

All the information in this book is to be used for informational and educational purposes only. The authors are not, in any way, responsible for any results that stem from the use of the contents herein. While conscious and creative attempts have been made to ensure that all information provided herein is as accurate and useful as possible, the author is not legally bound to be responsible for any damage caused by the accuracy as well as use/misuse of this information.

A special offer to those interested in this book

As a thank you for your interest in our book, we are offering a **free** report, "10 Commonly Used Terms in Artificial Intelligence". In this report, we'll identify and define 10 artificial intelligence terms that will help to prepare you for the era of AI.

For your free report on Artificial Intelligence, go to http://bit.ly/AIFreeReport

For Mom and Dad

Who always encouraged me to do my best, and for Michele, Daniel, and Michael to whom I am grateful for their love and support

Brian

To Mom & Dad

For the many trips to library and the gifts of reading and writing, and to Scott & Laura who taught me the meaning of the words "brother" and "sister"

Eric

TABLE OF CONTENTS

ABOUT

Do you feel overwhelmed by the complexities of the computer systems running your business? Do you have team members telling you that you've gone down the wrong path? Does it look like your business has been impacted adversely?

Leading technology has two meanings. The first, and the more obvious, relates to leading-edge technology. This may include advanced concepts like blockchain, artificial intelligence (AI), and the Internet of Things (IoT). Leading technology can also refer to guiding your organization through the implementation of fundamental technologies including business applications, productivity tools, and cyber security. In either case, integrating systems, departments, people, and process is a primary objective for many organizations in order to remain competitive or gain a competitive advantage over their industry peers.

Brian Iinuma has over 25 years' IT experience in Enterprise Resource Planning, payment processing, and direct marketing. He is the President and co-founder of Strategic Systems Group, Inc. (SSG), a provider of IT services to life sciences manufacturing and distribution companies. SSG's core competence is the implementation and support of ERP applications including Infor LN, Microsoft Dynamics, and SYSPRO. Mr. Iinuma serves as the Treasurer of the Southern California chapter of International Association of Microsoft Channel Partners and has made a series of technology presentations to the South Bay Chambers of Commerce, the Orange County chapter of SCORE, and a number of business associations. Mr. Iinuma is a #1 bestselling author and holds B.S. and MBA degrees from the University of California, Los Angeles.

Eric Klauss has over 20 years of experience selling, consulting and recommending business technology solutions, especially ERP & CRM as a customer, consultant, and salesperson in the industry. Today, he provides his sales and marketing expertise to PartnerSource Solutions clients and is a SCORE Mentor to business clients in Southern California. Eric, a #1 bestselling author, currently serves as Past President of the Southern California chapter of International Association of Microsoft Channel Partners (IAMCP) and West Region Chair for IAMCP – Americas.

INTRODUCTION

We live in a time of rapid change. To keep pace, manufacturing and distribution companies must understand and focus on *transformation to the intelligent enterprise.* It is a step-by-step, iterative process. Companies are racing to get there first in their respective industries. Where are you on that journey?

Let's begin with where you're at today. Selecting and implementing an Enterprise Resource Planning (ERP) system is a significant, yet important, undertaking for any manufacturing or distribution company. The ERP system touches nearly every aspect of the business, from sales and purchasing, to inventory control and manufacturing, to accounting and finance. Many people, internal and external to the organization, need to be involved to make the ERP system implementation and its ongoing operation successful. The cost is not insignificant. Yet, the benefits are many, including improved on-time delivery, optimal inventory carrying cost, reduced waste (e.g., material, human and financial resources), and powerful, visionary decisions that are "accurate-data-driven". Executives that embrace the technology and focus their companies' resources on successfully implementing an ERP system experience “Multiple Next-Levels Systems Evolution” and iterative improvement towards competitive advantage.

“12 Frequently Asked Questions About Enterprise Resource Planning Software” was written to address the most common questions we receive from executives about their organizations’ ERP systems. These questions touch on topics ranging from software selection to implementation to ongoing support issues. In this book, we’ll provide answers to 12 frequently asked questions that are likely to represent important issues in your organization and how to address them. Business owners, CEOs, CFOs, I/T executives, and middle managers responsible for sales, operations, and finance may benefit from reading this book.

Each chapter is intended to answer a frequently asked question about ERP systems and their implementation. In each chapter, there are key concepts and examples that provide additional detail and depth.

CHAPTER 1 – HOW TO SELECT AN ERP APPLICATION

What factors should a small or medium-sized business consider when selecting an ERP application?

As in many situations, the answer is often "It depends." Often, the type and size of organization and types of business processes are key factors.

Selecting the right software is a critical success factor in an ERP systems implementation. Many organizations face the tough decision of selecting the right ERP application that suits their type of business. In order to select the right ERP software, a number of factors should be considered. These include industry type, size of the organization, manufacturing process, the level of fit with the existing business processes, infrastructure, and technology, and the software will be used.

Industry Type

To obtain relevant information with which to make an informed decision, business owners and executives should ask questions like,

- "What software, including ERP applications, are business organizations using today?"
- "What is the size and nature of the primary business?"
- "Is there a unique vertical solution that addresses the company's largest market?"

If there is a vertical market product that fits the business perfectly, then despite the price premium compared to other solutions, an industry-specific ERP application might be the right one to implement.

In the late 1990s, we helped one of our clients select a replacement ERP application for his business. At the time, he had a choice between upgrading his current ERP application and implementing a different one. After some discussion about functionality, price, customization, and the level of effort required in each scenario, we concluded that implementing a different ERP application would be the most cost-effective solution.

Company Size

Because of the significant implementation costs involved, selecting the right ERP application is one of the most important decisions your executive team can make. When owners and executives realize that the business has outgrown the basic accounting solution it began with or when they find out that they have a lot of disparate Excel spreadsheets and silos of data (i.e., data repositories isolated from others), it's time to bring everything together into a single package. These are indications that executives should hasten the search for the right ERP software to fit the company's primary manufacturing processes.

Add a story: One client had been able to operate his business for many years using QuickBooks for financial reporting and Excel spreadsheets to manage the company's operations. The time came to migrate to a more comprehensive system. In the process of data migration, a number of discrepancies were identified. The client proposed that the new system was not functioning correctly. After closely analyzing a few of the discrepancies, the consulting team confirmed that the source data (i.e., the Excel spreadsheets) were in error. A formula error had been introduced several years prior to the migration and was propagated in subsequent periods. As a result, earnings for the business unit had to be restated, prompting the termination of the company's Chief Financial Officer.

Different kinds of applications will fit different sorts of companies. Company size is a big determinant of the kind and complexity of ERP application that should be implemented for the organization. In general, the larger the organization the more functionality (complexity) will be required. For instance, a small business using QuickBooks and spreadsheets to run its manufacturing organization will most likely not need a Tier 1 application (designed to service the needs of large, complex businesses with many departments and global locations) like SAP or Oracle because it will just be too big for the job. In cases like that, it would make more sense to choose a less complex package, because the leap from QuickBooks and spreadsheets to a Tier 2 (for divisions, subsidiaries and smaller locations of an organization) or Tier 3 ERP (serving smaller mid-sized companies offering fewer capabilities at reduced cost) application will be much more likely to succeed.

Fit with Existing Business Processes

Understanding your business processes goes a long way towards helping your organization chose the right ERP application. If your team members do not have a detailed understanding of the company's business processes and the way they work, they may have a hard time making the right choice. In order to overcome this challenge, team members must analyze the internal processes of the business and describe them in detail in writing. Because, regardless of what accounting or ERP solution is selected, the whole point is to bring those processes into one comprehensive system which can be used to operate the business. So, before making a choice of which solution to use, you must have your arms around the organization's core business processes.

The application should be selected so that it fits in with your existing business processes, or at least be very close. It is challenging to change the business process and the ERP application at the same time, but in many situations, that is exactly what your company may need to do. The company's executives and team members should review the business' processes to modify and streamline them before selecting an ERP application. If this process is done well, your team will stand a better chance of getting the system implemented.

Manufacturing Process

From an operational perspective, different manufacturing companies have different challenges. A company's primary manufacturing processes will have bearing on what ERP systems would be most suitable. For example, the applications that support process manufacturing could be quite different from those that support make-to-stock, make-to-order, and engineer-to-order operations, which would be radically different from a professional services or retail organization.

Fit with Existing Infrastructure and Technology

For most companies, instead of delving into using an ERP solution because others are using it, it is important to first assess the underlying technology. For instance, for a company using Microsoft Outlook for email and has a lot of data in Excel files, implementing a Microsoft solution or something equally deeply integrated will be a sensible choice to alleviate the need to manually transfer transactional data from one system to another.

In order to make an informed selection decision, organizations need to consider other start-up factors including:

- The underlying infrastructure of the company
- The system currently used to manage manufacturing and inventory

- The Customer Relationship Management (CRM) system currently in use
- Whether or not the CRM system should be integrated with the ERP solution in the future

Enterprise Considerations

Just like small and medium-sized organizations, large business enterprises are also faced with the challenge of selecting the right ERP package for their business. For instance, a division of a larger organization may have no choice but to use the same ERP application the parent company has implemented to maintain consistency with the rest of the organization.

One of our client contacts was recently promoted from a divisional I/T role to corporate. He asked us for help with two ERP systems migrations to the corporate standard, SAP. On the surface, this appears to be a straightforward task. However, each of the divisions has its own ERP system supporting business operations well. In addition, there are dozens of third-party applications and customizations that need to be analyzed to determine if they need to be migrated to corporate's SAP environment.

However, on occasion, we've observed situations where the corporate ERP application does not support the division's business model and processes well. In such cases, it makes more sense for the division to choose an ERP system that fits its business and just report financial data to the parent organization.

Reporting Requirements

Another level of complexity in the ERP system selection process relates to reporting capabilities. In certain cases, especially in businesses with specialized operations, the reporting requirements drive the selection of the ERP application. Unlike earlier systems when accounting applications did not have much of business processes incorporated into them, today's applications come with a lot of business intelligence or data warehouse functionality that has been proven to be sufficient for many small to medium-sized organizations. However, in the case of larger organizations which might be a division of a corporate entity and separate from a financial perspective, sometimes the division would have to deal with multi-company, multi-location, or multi-currency requirements; hence the process becomes even more complex, elevating the requirements of the ERP application.

Chapter Summary

In Chapter 1, we covered selecting an ERP application. In situations where an industry-specific ERP application is available, this system should be considered. Company size, fit with existing manufacturing processes and technology infrastructure, and reporting requirements should be considered in the software selection process.

CHAPTER 2 - IMPLEMENTATION COST AND TIMING

A typical client generates approximately $25 M in revenue and has about 60 users. For such a client, how much time and how much money would be required to implement a new ERP application?

To answer this question appropriately, several components of cost must be considered.

It is important to look at all elements of cost when considering an ERP system implementation or migration. Hardware (virtual and physical), software, and implementation services are the most obvious components. In addition, the less obvious components include internal resources, time away from day-to-day operations of the business, and unforeseen impacts on product delivery, customer service, and the collection of cash.

Hardware and Software

When considering an ERP application for a company with about 60 users and $25 million in revenue, the obvious costs include hardware and software licensing. However, at this size range, the larger part of the cost of bringing in a new solution is going to be the cost of implementation. In general, the cost of implementation will be somewhat higher relative to the cost of the software. At this size range, the low end of basic implementation may be around $20,000. However, to address specific business or industry requirements, companies may decide to implement much more complex and expensive solutions. The primary objective to keep in mind is to meet multiple needs of your business. Depending on the situation, this may involve bringing in ancillary solutions like Electronic Data Interchange (EDI), document management, and manufacturing or distribution solutions, and barcode scanning solutions. In the case of a manufacturing organization, other solutions that may need to be brought in include sales tax compliance, field service management, project accounting, and document management solutions. There is a lot of functionality that can be added to the core ERP solution, but these applications designed to provide that much more in the way of automation, increased productivity, and enhanced visibility of information for the ownership and leadership teams. At enterprise level or a division of an enterprise level corporation, in many cases, the hardware is a relatively small component of the overall cost and the software is more significant. As a rule of the thumb, the cost is in the range of $4,000 to $5,000 per user to purchase the license for the software at the outset. At $5,000 per user, the software cost for 60 users would be about $300,000. Another cost that is somewhat less easy to estimate is the cost of implementation services.

Implementation Services

Generally, organizations that purchase an ERP application will not implement it on their own. This is because internal personnel generally do not have the time or are not qualified to do it and will turn the implementation into a very costly undertaking. Due to the complexity of the software and the skills necessary to implement it, they will most likely need to engage the services of a consulting firm that is well-versed in the application they are implementing. The service provider will then undertake the process of planning, implementation, and support.

To get all these done, the implementation cost could be the same as or up to twice the cost of the software. For example, if the hardware and software licenses cost $300,000, the implementation services might cost about 1.5 times that amount. The overall cost of hardware, software, and services could be $600,000 to $750,000 and could approach a million dollars in larger organizations. While these numbers seem daunting, engaging an experienced consulting firm will save you time and money. A rapid implementation allows clients to get a faster return on their investment. Highly skilled project managers and consultants guide the project using best practices, eliminating wasted effort and, more importantly, time fixing mistakes.

These ratios of software cost to services are somewhat "old school". In today's modern "cloud" world they may not be directly applicable; it really comes down to the time it takes to implement. For example, a small company might migrate to a new cloud-based solution and pay $100-$300 per user per month for 10 users. In this scenario, the old idea of using a ratio between software license cost and implementation services is no longer applicable. To migrate data, tailor the new system to the firm's business process and, do some element of training, you will need to look at somewhere between $10,000 and $100,000 in services, depending on the nature of the organization and the complexity of the organization's requirements. Some people might wonder why there is such a wide range. It will depend on the focused effort internal personnel are able to allocate to the project. We'll talk about Software as a Service (SaaS) solutions and time to implement shortly.

However, it is important to note that the cost of implementing an ERP application for a manufacturing company is always higher than for a distribution company. For instance, if a small manufacturing company is going to expend about $100,000 to get a new system in place, it is not uncommon for the cost for an implementation in a distribution company to be $75,000 to $80,000. One of our clients manufactures large pieces of equipment for the packaging industry. The manufacturing process is especially intricate because of the need to configure the product before manufacture. During the migration process we expended a significant amount of time translating the configuration bills of material to a format useable in the new system. Another of our clients is a distributor of apparel and related products. Manufacturing is outsourced to firms in China, so the client's new system only needs to set up to track orders for products purchased for resale.

Cost of Internal Resources

The cost of internal resources required for implementing a new ERP application may be a little difficult to quantify. Lots of I/T resources get consumed in this process and departments that will be affected by in the implementation of the application will also need to be involved. For example, subject matter experts from Operations, Finance, Inventory Control, Sales, and Purchasing will be needed to support the implementation.

Time to Implement

Some organizations expect their new ERP system to be installed and running in 3 weeks, others 3 months, but those timeframes are rarely attainable. Three months might be enough time to get some of the planning done before getting started with the implementation. It is possible to get something up and running in about 3 months in situations where there is no system already in place. However, if the company has an existing ERP application and existing processes, all of which are fairly well-tuned, the implementation time could be easily twice or triple that. It is important for companies to realize how much elapsed time and how much effort from their internal resources are going to be required.

To some degree, the timing and cost is dependent on the organization and how much effort its leadership is willing to invest. For organizations who want to implement themselves, or who are willing to take on a vast majority of the implementation, the cost of implementation goes down significantly. However, the flipside is that the client may not always have personnel that can be dedicated 100% to the project. This is because organizations do not have team members waiting in the wings to tackle a project like this. The personnel in the company who can undertake this, whether in the Sales, Operations, or the Finance departments of the company, have other jobs to do; they cannot be totally dedicated to this project. The best they can do is to put some part-time effort into the project, and that is not enough for the kind of tasks involved. If a company can only invest 10% of its human resources into the implementation, that will significantly limit the ability of the service provider to get on with the project, much less deliver on time. Even though there are many things that the service provider can do, there are still tasks that the client has to be responsible for in any implementation. It is a team effort and, in order to get the job done, the service provider requires the client's interaction. In general, it is always advisable to encourage team members who are going to operate a new ERP application to adopt it.

The implementation takes longer and costs more money if:

- Internal personnel are stuck to the existing process or unfamiliar with the new one
- Training was insufficient

- There were mistakes in the data migration or system configuration that weren't identified in pilot testing

Often, the fault lies not with the software provider or the consulting firm, but the organization's internal personnel.

Change Management

Change management is the approach or process to prepare team members in making a significant organizational change. Without doubt, implementing an ERP application qualifies as a significant organizational change. It is critical for the organization to understand the change management aspects of bringing in a new ERP solution or any other business solution. If the users are unwilling to change, and if the senior management is not engaged in ensuring the change process is successful, the project is going to be very difficult.

If the users fail to embrace and take advantage of the training or don't commit themselves to learning the new solution, no matter how much time the consulting firm or software provider invests, the project will be difficult to execute to completion.

The inability or unwillingness of the users to learn and adjust to the new system typically means that the consultants must start teaching the process afresh and this would delay the go-live process.

Software as a Service

Software as a Solution (SaaS) emerged with the early computing technology of the 1960s. In that era, IBM and other mainframe providers established a service bureau business, also referred to as time-sharing or utility computing. Today, SaaS is often used interchangeably with cloud computing. Thanks to the Internet and global communications, SaaS applications span many industries including modern business applications like ERP.

Many clients have questions about SaaS solutions, their cost, and time to implement. The truth is that many vendors and publishers are out there, trying to get clients to buy their software. In some cases, clients spend hundreds of thousands of dollars on software licensing. As you might guess, this becomes a deterrent to many organizations. Vendors seems to have universally evaluated this situation and developed SaaS or SaaS-like solution. SaaS solutions are typically sold on monthly subscription basis. Hence, instead of spending $300,000 on software licensing, subscribers only have to pay about $300 per user per month. This presents a great opportunity for the vendors to attract a large number of clients, but the burden would still lie in the cost of implementation.

NetSuite and Microsoft Dynamics 365 are examples of applications that are considered to be SaaS, while many other applications are following on the same path. From a financial perspective, by defining a narrow scope of work, the consultant may choose to make the upfront cost for services relatively modest since the hardware and software have already been provided by another party for a monthly fee.

From a standpoint of functionality, the critical factor is not whether it is SaaS or is hosted some place in the cloud. What does matter is the system's functionality and how well it fits into the business processes.

There are clients with in-house servers, in place since 2011 especially, who have heard a lot about the cloud and want to go to the cloud. These clients want a SaaS or cloud-based solution, and if they find a product that is fit for them, that would be perfect. However, the challenge with the SaaS licensing model is that it doesn't change the amount of time it takes for the solution to be implemented. Essentially, only the cost structure for acquiring the license has be changed into a monthly cost, but the complexity of the solution and the amount of time required for implementation has not changed. The significant thing is that after the application has been moved to a cloud-based solution, there will no longer be a need to install and maintain software on a local physical server. However, that is just a small fraction when compared to the time clients will need for the overall implementation of an ERP solution. This is one of the challenges for many mid-market customers, as they don't understand that although the cost structure has changed, the time required for the implementation has not eliminated. This is a piece of information the SaaS vendors do not tell customers as they explain how easy it is to deploy their applications. The truth is, that despite the change in payment structure, the services requirement doesn't change; significant time and effort is still required from the service provider and internal personnel within the organization.

Chapter Summary

In Chapter 2, we reviewed implementation cost and timing. Hardware, software, and consulting costs are pretty easy to identify. Estimating the internal costs, specifically human resources, is sometimes more difficult. The overall cost of the implementation should be weighed against the expected benefits. Underestimating the time to implement has a number of adverse ramifications, including the possibility of selecting a sub-optimal set of resources for the implementation.

CHAPTER 3 - DATA MIGRATION

What does a data migration from an old to a new ERP application entail?

There are several considerations and, if this is not done correctly, the implementation process will be much more difficult.

Data migration involves taking the data from an old ERP application to a new one. It is very important to apply adequate resources to the data migration. Furthermore, it is critical to validate that the data is migrated accurately during the pilot test phase, because going into production with faulty or incomplete data can create a daunting situation for the entire organization.

Responsibility for the Integrity of the Data

Ultimately, clients are responsible for the integrity of the data. They have to be able to own their data and understand it so well that they can guide I/T personnel to load the data in right places. Clients also need to be involved in terms of answering vital questions. For example, when loading phone numbers, the client needs to confirm that everyone used dashes or if some people used parentheses or periods in the phone number upon data entry. If these irregularities are not handled properly, there could be a giant problem when the you go live on the system. Inconsistent use inside the existing system is another challenge, which will necessitate a cleanup in the data migration process.

Some of the newer ERP applications, released in the past three years, have data intelligence built into them. For example, when the data migration of a phone number occurs, the application can detect irregularities so that they can be corrected without a separate data cleanup task. One tactic that may be appropriate is to load summary data without the corresponding detail. This commonly occurs with General Ledger (G/L) data, which has a large number of component transactions. Clients sometimes choose to migrate the G/L data at a summary level, including balances for each account by month, to the new ERP application rather than trying to load all the underlying detail. This requires the client's accounting team to do a monthly, quarterly, or year-end comparison on a transaction basis, which doesn't make a lot of sense. Loading G/L data at a summary level is helpful if the value of the detail data is in question.

Which Data to Migrate

The data migration can be classified into different segments: 1) static master data, 2) open transactions and 3) transaction history. The static master data is the simplest. This includes the bills of material, routings, and data that pertain to customers and vendors. The next simplest segment is open transactions including open sales orders, open purchase orders, and open production orders. Transaction history, such as transaction-by-transaction sales, purchase and production order history, pose a great challenge during the migration process.

When possible, instead of migrating historical data, consultants will encourage clients to consider an archive or a data warehouse solution. For the data that are transactional in nature, having access to the old system for a period of time or a data warehouse containing the transactional data often turns out to be a better solution than migrating historical transactions into the new ERP application. The client benefits by not spending money on migrating data with relatively low value (i.e., records that will be needed infrequently). Training users to transact sales, purchase, and production orders in a newly migrated company is generally a straightforward task.

Length of Time Historical Data Need to be Maintained

Clients always as us how long they should maintain their historical data. It is relatively rare to lose access to historical data. However, if that is the case, it is normal and reasonable to move the data into a data warehouse. But the other realization is that, to some degree, that data is not going to be important in a year or two after going live on the new system. By that time, that data may be useless. There aren't too many organizations, especially small and mid-market companies who do look back and do financial analysis going back more than 12 to 24 months. Most of these companies are growing so quickly that what they did 3 to 5 years ago isn't very relevant to the way they are running their business today. So, in most cases, there is not much value in bringing over all the historical data.

For many clients, 12 months of historical data, which is inexpensive from a data migration standpoint, is enough to perform a year-over-year review, month-to-month comparisons, and similar analysis.

The Overall Cost of Data Migration

The cost of data migration depends mainly on the type of data to be migrated and what tools used are used in the migration process. These factors determine migration cost even with QuickBooks. For example, a client in the medical equipment manufacturing industry, once wanted to migrate data from a QuickBooks Online solution. She wanted to migrate all the data to a new solution, including the line item details within the G/L. Most, if not all, of the solutions on the market today do not have a migration tool that can get to that level of transaction detail. Migrating the historical G/L detail entails taking monthly or quarterly snapshots of the company's financials. However, this client wanted all the transaction details migrated over to the new solution. So, when the service providers discussed the requirement with the software vendor and gave the client a quote of about $10,000, the client said it was expensive and decided to go on a personal search for a cheaper solution. She went online and got someone who said he could do it for $5,000, half of the price the first consultant quoted. The second vendor began the project for the client, but within a relatively short period of time, the original estimate of the effort went out the window. The client had already spent, at that point in time, the original $5,000, but the vendor kept coming back to demand more money until the client ended up spending about $20,000 for the data migration.

The client ended up spending two times what she was originally quoted by the first consultants. It became a no-win situation for the consultants because they could not tell their client, "I told you so." even though they really wanted to.

The company ultimately did go live, but the amount of time it took to get through that data migration was almost twice the time initially estimated. Further, the overall project was much delayed, and its total cost was quite a bit larger than expected, which made the client very unhappy. That was one of those worst-case scenarios of how things can go badly in a data migration project. When things go great, the implementation team just looks at it and says that it's simple. But to be realistic, it's never simple.

The Costs of an Incorrect or Incomplete Data Migration

We were brought into a situation where the data migration project was done poorly. What was perceived to be a training issue was actually a data migration problem. The sales orders that were supposed to be open and have historical information were transferred haphazardly. As a result, the users were not able to ship their sales orders out, send invoices to customers, and collect cash. Ultimately, the client encountered some financial difficulty as a result of those delays. The consultants were willing to help them get past some of those difficulties, but the correct solution was for the client to go back to the original provider and ask for the additional time or free consulting get to be able to resume normal operations. Financially, the client suffered a great deal before getting things straightened out. Data migration has, on the surface, a very straightforward nature, however, if not done properly, it could have very serious financial implications.

Migration Tools

Migration from QuickBooks is probably the most commonly used solution for small businesses. Many vendors of ERP software have created tools to enable the migration of some of that data to the new solution, making the process relatively easy. In many situations, ERP applications have data import tools to provide a way to utilize data from various sources, including Excel spreadsheets.

Data Cleanup Prior to or During Migration

One thing clients often fail to take note of is that there is a data cleanup task that needs to be completed, and it has to be done by them. Service providers and consultants may extract data and normalize the data for the new system, but that's just data. They just look at it, make sure that things appear the way they should. For instance, they ensure that an address looks like an address, a phone number looks like a phone number, and a zip code looks like a zip code. The consultants look at those things and make sure that they appear as they should, however, if the client has an item number in an item description field or if the client uses another field within the system for something else completely, the consultants may not notice that.

Benefits of a Data Warehouse in Data Migration

Our consultants once helped a Department of Defense subcontractor migrate from a legacy ERP application on to software that was well-accepted by their corporate headquarters. A legacy application is computer system that is in operation past its useful life. The migration process turned out to be straightforward. There was no need to do a lot of data migration work because the client already had a data warehouse solution that we provided to them years prior. Hence, the process of using the data warehouse to complete the migration to the new ERP application was relatively simple.

Chapter Summary

In Chapter 3, we reviewed migrating the data from the old to the new application. Ultimately the client has the responsibility for the integrity of the data. Selecting which data to migrate (i.e., master data, open transactions, transaction history) will directly influence the cost of the data migration. There is an opportunity to clean up the data in the process of data migration. A data warehouse may be helpful in the process of data migration and providing a repository for the data in the old system.

CHAPTER 4 – ACTIVITIES DURING AN IMPLEMENTATION

What activities should clients expect during an ERP system implementation?

There are many activities, internal and external to the organization, that need to be addressed.

These activities need to be identified, documented, and executed in the process of implementation. A planning document with milestones is useful to define what needs to be accomplished and keeps the project team on track. In general, organizations perform well by completing one milestone before moving on to the next. It also gives your team a feeling of accomplishment as milestones are completed.

Activity 1: Conduct a Discovery in the Office

The first phase of most projects is to explore some elements of a deeper-dive discovery process in the client's organization. Consultants get in, under the covers, to review the organization's internal business processes, and begin to map out what will be the new ERP solution. To do this, the consultant must interact with both the senior executive team and the key personnel who are responsible for critical points in various business processes within the organization. For instance, in a manufacturing organization, an implementation would require an interaction with Controller and Chief Financial Officer along with key personnel in Operations and Sales.

Activity 2: Conduct A Discovery on the Shop Floor

The next phase is to look at the key personnel from the side of the organization's warehouse and manufacturing operations and the people who take responsibility for the shipping and receiving of inventory to identify their information requirements. In many cases, personnel in sales and marketing departments will need information from production at the end of the day. For example, they need to know when they can sell, from where they can sell it, and how long products will be in production before being available for sale. These requirements are important to define an overall solution. The essential part from the consulting side is to understand all the complexities in the client's business processes.

Activity 3: Planning Document with Milestones

Here is an example of how to chart your implementation process.

Typically, the implementation process has milestones like:

Milestone	Related Activity
Business Process Analysis	Reviewing and documenting the organization's business processes
Project Planning	Identifying the tasks necessary to complete the project and assigning responsibility and timeframes to complete them
Software Development / Enhancement	Modifying or customizing the system to accommodate specialized business processes or increase user adoption
Unit Testing	Testing by the software developers to verify that the software enhancements meet the technical

	specifications
User Acceptance Testing	Testing by the users of the system to validate that the software enhancements meet the requirements of the project
Pilot Test 1 (with manually keyed data)	Testing all aspects of the new system using manually keyed data
Pilot Test 2 (with migrated data)	Testing all aspects of the new system using data migrated from the old system
Training	Training of the end users by key project team members
Documentation	Document business processes and high-level and detailed "desk" procedures

Go Live	Transition from the old to the new ERP system
Post-Implementation Support	Address any issues that arise after the new system has been implemented

These should be included in a planning document with start dates, due dates, responsibility, and status. Tools like Microsoft Projects are very helpful in developing an implementation plan, however, in many cases, a detailed Excel spreadsheet will suffice.

Activity 4: Documentation of Existing Business Process

Developing a roadmap for the implementation has some similarities to planning software development. Drawing certain aspects from lean programming methodology and incorporating them into the implementation has some distinct benefits. For example, the discovery process enables the project team to look at the business as a whole and gives it a chance to critically evaluate and document specific business processes. From there, the team can begin the process of mapping the data collection points, defining the work flow, and fitting the business processes into the functionality of the new solution.

Activity 5: Assess Whether Business Processes Fit with System Functionality

It is critical to make an assessment regarding how well the business processes fit with the ERP application. At this point, the team has the chance to develop a plan for execution, similar to a specifications document in software development. The plan may include eliminating inefficient business processes so that the project team can see how the new system can be used to make the operation more efficient.

Activity 6: Reengineer the Business Processes

In the beginning of an implementation project, the project team may need to reengineer some of the workarounds that were implemented because of limitations of the current system. Instead of forcing the old processes into the new system, there is an opportunity for the consulting team to explore those processes with the client and potentially to reengineer them to take advantage of the new system or a more effective way of completing the work. It may involve some other technology as well. For example, in a distribution or a manufacturing environment, the team might consider bringing in barcode scanning application as a part of the project. This can radically change some of the requirements for inventory management.

One of our client engagements involved automating the calculation of the standard costs of electronic components manufactured offshore. In addition to automating the manual spreadsheet processes, it was necessary to analyze the manufacturing processes as well. While many were acceptable as they were, several, because of recent innovations, were revised to combine two final packaging steps, reducing both manufacturing time and cost.

Business process reengineering is an important part of the overall solution implementation. Once done, the newly defined business processes must be tested to confirm that they are going to be more efficient than the existing processes. These are all critical customer tasks that cannot be done in absentia. During business process engineering, the consultants should not be working independently without coordinating with your project team.

Activity 7: Allocate All Needed Resources

This is a team project. Resources from the client's team and from the consulting firm must work together as a tightly integrated unit. This is needed to ultimately bring a complete solution, that meets the needs of the organization, to fruition. In other words, at the final go-live phase, there is a smooth transition from the old to the new ERP solution.

Activity 8: Create Documentation

Documentation falls into two broad categories. One is related to the business processes, including swim lanes and flow diagrams, that document how processes are supposed to be executed. This category also includes how system processes should be mapped into the business process.

The other category is procedural documentation, often written at a high level. However, often, there is also a need for detailed "desk" procedures that describe specific steps for team members to process transactions in the new system. These are sometimes referred to as Standard Operating Procedures (SOPs) or a "How to Reference Guide".

In both categories, documentation is important to the organization. In the first, which involves mapping out business processes, documenting those processes is also a part of the step of validating them with the client's team. Members of the consulting team must map those processes out, as they understand them from the client's perspective.

In this way, the consulting team can reproduce the business processes in written form, so that the customer can review, understand, and validate them. This a key step before the project team infuses the business processes into the workflow of the new system. It is also critical for the client's team to look at what has been done, indicate whether things are being done correctly, and communicate whether a step was missed. It is necessary for the consultants to understand all the details correctly and the optimal way to understand them is to document them.

Activity 9: Train End-Users

There is a need for understanding and skillfulness on the part of the end users of the new system. This can be obtained through reading training guides, handbooks, or system documentation. Some organizations choose to train their personnel, but some do not. This kind of investment, in fact, can pay off with big dividends for organizations in the long run. The potential downside of not training manifests itself when a key member of the project team leaves the organization during the implementation or shortly afterwards. This is compounded if she does not transfer the knowledge to her successor. When the successor takes up the role of the departing team member but does not know what his basic job is or how to execute it, a retraining process must be undertaken at this point. This retraining process increases the cost of implementation in most cases. However, having a training guide or procedural documentation on hand can alleviate some of the stress and unnecessary expense. There will be a smoother succession if there is some baseline transfer of knowledge.

Chapter Summary

In Chapter 4, we reviewed the activities typically executed in an ERP system implementation. These activities include planning, business process analysis, business process reengineering, training, and documentation. One of the more important activities is pilot testing, since errors in data migration or transaction processing procedures will have a significant impact when the organization goes live on the new system.

CHAPTER 5 - COMMON ISSUES DURING IMPLEMENTATION

What kinds of issues commonly arise during an ERP system implementation?

The variety of issues that could arise is pretty broad. They range from data migration problems to overlooked "shadow" business processes to user adoption. If these can be identified and planned for in the analysis stage, the implementation will go more smoothly.

Issue 1: The Scope of the Project Changes Significantly

Change in the scope of the project is most likely going to be the most significant issue. It comes because of exposure to the capabilities in the new system.

It is like bringing in a piece of new technology that has a thousand bells and whistles to it. However, the organization was only expecting to deploy a hundred of those bells and whistles.

Then as the customer becomes more exposed to the capabilities of the system they may see something they like.

However, it wasn't part of the initial requirements. It wasn't part of the wish list. It's something that they didn't even know could be part of the solution, but now they see it in the system and they want it.

As an example, in one client engagement, we agreed to limit the scope of a field service implementation to the capture and transfer of service order data and related financial reporting. As the project progressed, more detailed reporting requirements were surfaced. We executed a project change order to address a portion of the requirements. Fortunately, our data warehouse for the service module was adequate to address the balance of the reporting requirements.

It's like when you go new car shopping and are exposed to a backup camera on a new car. If you've never had a backup camera before, you will not think that it's that much of a requirement. Because you've driven for 20 years without a backup camera before and you've never had an accident, you may ask if you really need one of those. You get in the car the first time and you put the car in reverse, and suddenly, you see the backup camera. Perhaps, it's a life-changing moment when you realize, "Wow, I really love this technology. I love the fact that I can see what's going on behind me. I want and need that now."

Something akin to this often happens during the implementation. When a new requirement pops up from nowhere, there becomes a question for the organization, "What do we do? Do we implement this now or wait for Phase 2?"

Issue 2: The Cost and Timing Estimates Were Too Optimistic

When there is a new project, there is a budget allocated to it. So, the question is, "Can we fit this new item into the original budget?" It is possible in some cases. However, if not, the project team must make a decision either to remove something else from the scope in order to fit the new requirement in or to add extra resources in the form of money and time to the project. It is a decision that the project and executive teams within the customer's organization must make together.

Issue 3: The Impact on Internal Personnel Was Larger Than Expected

While the consulting team can certainly help, internal resources, especially from subject matter experts are critical to the success of the implementation. 25% to 30% is probably a good estimate of time required to complete the project in a timely fashion. Staff turnover is certainly a situation where issues are likely to arise during implementation.

Issue 4: Unforeseen Gaps Between Business Processes and System Functionality

In many cases business processes and functions were put in place based on the prior system or the prior process, even if it was a paper-based process. There were some rules and some boundaries put in place about the way that things were supposed to be done. When bringing in a new piece of technology for the organization, gaps are bound to exist between the business processes and the system's functionality. These can be addressed by reengineering the business processes or enhancing the system.

Issue 5: Inadequate Processes to Manage Change within the Organization

Change management is a discipline that defines how companies prepare and support team members to successfully adopt change and create organizational success. Managing change in a company is one of the biggest challenges that arises during an implementation. In general, how well the organization manages change is a critical success factor in such projects.

Issue 6: Biting Off More Than the Organization Can Chew

Biting off more than the organization can chew, in this context, refers to "over-implementation" or "overreaching" during an implementation. In general, if it is possible, the way to address this is to take on an initial phase, get that squared away, and then take on a Phase 2. Often, things go a little better than trying to complete the work in Phases 1 and 2 in one shot. It's like eating a meal in courses: salad, main course, then dessert. A phased implementation can sometimes work better, especially if the organization doesn't have spare human resources internally. If the number of people who can apply themselves to completing an implementation is relatively small, it's often better to do things in small chunks as opposed to large. From a cost-benefit perspective, organizations can derive the benefits of the Phase 1 functionality, while working on Phase 2.

Issue 7: Incomplete or Incorrect Data Migration

As stated earlier, there are situations where the data migration is not up to specification or the data migration process is not completed on time. This situation often arises when organizations try to complete tasks in parallel with the hope that they dovetail at the right time for a pilot test. Sometimes the timing doesn't quite work out, or maybe the migration team does finish what it thinks is correct, but when it finally comes down to testing, the data entry and reporting processes just fail. The sales orders won't ship, you can't get the invoices out, and you can't collect cash all because data migration was done incorrectly.

Issue 8: Not Including Accounting until the End of the Implementation

Finance is often the last functional area to get a handle on what's happening in the system. Unfortunately, or fortunately, all roads lead to Finance. At the end of the day, within most organizations, things boil down to either time or money and that's the purview of the Controller and the CFO. How those resources, whether it's time or money, are allocated is driven back to the Controller and the CFO. Although they don't necessarily hold primary responsibility for the allocation of those resources, they do have responsibility for reporting the use of those resources.

Quite often, the difficulties for Finance come from the manufacturing end of the ERP application. The sales orders, purchase orders, accounts receivable, and accounts payable, generally flow into the general ledger well. However, when it comes down to inventory control, receipts of material against purchase orders, movement of inventory from location to location, issues of inventory to production orders, and receipts from production orders into finished goods, the flow of data becomes less clear. The calculations of purchasing and manufacturing variances become the bane of Accounting and no one really understands them, except for Accounting. One of the interesting things that we've observed is that many team members within the organization don't understand the complete process. Exceptions are typically found in the Finance organization where some personnel actually have a good perspective on what that overall process really does look like from point to point within the organization.

Chapter Summary

In Chapter 5, we covered common issues that arise during an ERP system implementation, including significant changes in scope, problems with the data migration, and unexpected demands on internal personnel. One of the most impactful issues is not having adequate change management processes in place during the implementation.

CHAPTER 6 – ENGAGING A CONSULTING FIRM FOR IMPLEMENTATION

Why should firms consider engaging a consulting firm to assist during an ERP system implementation?

It often comes down to not having enough available internal human resources.

Without some level of consulting support, it is very difficult to learn the application, execute the implementation tasks, and manage day-to-day activities all at the same time. Also, there is often justification to temporarily engage additional staff-level resources to support day-to-day activities while the implementation is under way.

Reasons to Do It Yourself

If you have the resources and the knowledge to implement the solution entirely by yourself, then you don't need a consulting organization. However, we have encountered literally one scenario where a client implemented its ERP system completely by itself. It was a function of the COO of the organization, a brilliant guy, who had graduated from

UCLA with a master's degree in computer science. He was the son of one of the owners and they spent the time to implement the solution. It took about 9 months to implement the solution. To put that into perspective, with a consulting organization helping, an implementation of that nature would typically be completed in 3 to 4 months.

If there is sufficient knowledge available within the organization to implement on your own, then it is reasonable to go ahead and try that. In another case, a prospective client, a relatively small service organization, with one person in the finance area, decided to go it alone. She was contemplating implementing an ERP application, but just the accounting portion, in the organization. She had worked with this program before and she understood the chart of accounts structure very well. She could basically do all the work herself, perhaps with a little of help on the technical side. Conceptually, she could do the entire implementation herself without much consulting help at all.

At the other end of the spectrum, some clients that are large, enterprise-sized organizations can implement themselves. In one case, a client had an I/T staff of 35, which is the size of some small businesses. The team members had quite a lot of experience in supported ERP applications and could essentially implement on their own.

In a last case, the client was a division of a larger parent organization. The parent organization was in a similar situation, where it had a significant number of I/T personnel on staff, all well-versed in the same ERP application. As divisions come up on this application, the corporate office sent out teams of people to get these implementations going and, in terms of consulting resources, the client needed very little help from the outside. Our role for this particular client was basically to get some data off of the legacy application in a format that could be imported in the new system. After that, corporate resources completed the rest of the work. It was amazing.

Reason 1: Time to Implementation

In the first example, above, it took twice as much of the organization time to implement that solution. It was, however, a choice that the client made.

Let's use an analogy, a couple retired several years ago, and decided to go and build a house on their own. They had inherited some land and they wanted to build a house on the land. The husband was retiring and had some prior experience and background in the construction industry.

So, he had some knowledge but he'd never done anything like this himself before. He thought it'd be a fun hobby. They went ahead and started the process of constructing their home. They originally estimated that it would take them about a year to build the home. They began the process and they were living in a little mobile home on the property while they were going through the construction.

They had the time, they had the resources, and they also felt that doing it themselves would save them a bunch of money. That was their perspective going into it. In the end, their original estimate of the time to complete of one year was closer to five years. When they finally got the house finished, cost of the overall construction was two times what it had originally been estimated. The couple, in the process of building, realized they didn't have all the knowledge that they needed and ended up bringing in some contractors along the way to do parts of the construction. So, in the end, their cost ended up being double their original budget for the project and their time investment was almost 5 times of their original estimate. This is the kind of challenge that exists in ERP systems implementations.

The following chart illustrates the typical division of responsibilities between the client and consulting teams:

Client Responsibilities	Service Provider Responsibilities	Resulting Action Item
Provide access to Subject Matter Experts (SMEs), usually key managers and supervisors	Gather available documentation and requirements for the new ERP system	Discovery document and implementation plan
Define and document existing business processes	Review existing businesses process and identify gaps	Map existing business processes into functionality of the new ERP system
Identify and document key business requirements of the ERP new system	Review requirements and identify missing components	Identify possible sources of missing functionality, including 3rd party applications

		and custom software development
Provide access to the existing system and related data	Review existing data structures and content	Map data from the old into the new ERP system
Testing: User acceptance and pilot testing	Unit testing of various software components, coordinate user acceptance and pilot testing	Identify and address any gaps in functionality or new requirements
Training: Allocate key personnel who will be in training and designated to train others in their functional areas	Provide training to key personnel in all functional areas impacted by the new system	Create high level procedural documentation
Documentation: Provide detailed	If needed, developed desk	Validate documentation

procedural documentation for all personnel responsible for the transition from table to the new ERP system	procedures for personnel responsible for data entry	with results of pilot tests
Go live: Allocate all necessary resources to transition from the old to the new ERP system	Observe operation of the new system to ensure that it is working as expected	Identify and, as quickly as possible, address the issues that may arise after going live

Reason 2: Overall Cost of Implementation

You can do it yourself, but you may find that, in fact, you don't save any money and you certainly don't do it any faster. And that's the challenge. You are not gaining the benefits of the solution that you've selected as quickly as you need to. Part of the calculation of bringing in a new solution is the return on your investment. In other words, "How quickly can I achieve a return on the investment that I'm making or bringing in new technology." Regardless of what that technology is, whether it's ERP or CRM or something else, what is important is that simple Return on Investment (ROI) calculation. The longer it takes to attain that ROI, the less valuable it is to the organization. In part, that's just driven by the time value of money. In other words, the value of a dollar today is actually higher than the value of a dollar three years from now.

Hiring a consultant helps you reduce the cost of implementation and reap the benefits sooner.

Reason 3: Insufficient Internal Human Resources

Having knowledge and experience is essential, but the challenge is that in most organizations, you have people that have already have full-time jobs. They are a Controller, an Accountant, a Manufacturing Supervisor, or a Warehouse Manager. Whatever their job functions may be they have a full-time job already. Your company is paying them a salary and potentially some additional compensation above and beyond that. But since they already have a full-time job, how much additional time do they have to put towards the implementation of new technology? Maybe that's 10%; maybe that's 20%. In many cases, that's about as much as is obtainable in most organizations. Full-time employees could potentially put in 45 or 50 hours in a week. Maybe they could dedicate five to ten of those hours towards the implementation of a new solution. That's about it. So, the time dedicated determines how quickly companies can embrace the new solution, how quickly the employees can bring that return to the organization, and how quickly they can get started with that goal and realizing the benefits of it.

Chapter Summary

In Chapter 6, we outlined reasons to engage with a consulting resource to support the implementation. Insufficient internal resources, a steep learning curve, and total cost of ownership are primary factors. Also, a consulting team can help to shorten the implementation time, allowing the client organization to realize a return on its investment more quickly than it otherwise would have.

CHAPTER 7 - MANAGING THE DATA IN THE OLD SYSTEM

What have clients typically done with the data in the systems they are migrating from?

Regarding the data in the previous system, there are a few decisions to make. Often the approach will depend on the organization's assessment of future requirements.

The issue of what to do with data from the previous system has a few facets. Often the answer depends on:

- What the client expects to use this data for
- How long it needs to be available
- The budget available to put a solution in place

For example, if the data is only required for reporting purposes, a data warehouse might be the best. If there are regulatory requirements (e.g., FDA, HIPPA, etc.), a working read-only version of the old system might be the most sensible solution. In the discussion that follows, we'll touch on these tradeoffs and present solutions.

Maintain the Old System

The old system still matters to some extent. Flipping the switch and moving everybody over to the new system does not make the old system automatically vaporize. In most cases, it is still going to continue operating in one form or another. If for instance, we are talking about a QuickBooks system, it is probably on someone's desktop somewhere. If the data is there and if there is a need to do a look back for some reason, organizations can certainly do that. The flipside to this is that the value of that data diminishes over time. It's not like wine. It doesn't get better with age. So, from the standpoint of usability, in the first few months of the new system being live, the data in the old system will be of some value. However, it wouldn't be cost-effective for the consulting team to invest tons of time and effort because a client might need the data one day. Over time, say a year or two later, the data is probably not going to have a whole lot of value.

Data Warehouse

There may be legacy transactional data that is not to be migrated to the new system. However, if there is a desire to have access to that transactional data in the future, then one option is to migrate them into a data warehouse. A data warehouse is simply a database that stores information from the old system in a user-friendly format. This serves two purposes: 1) storage of the historical information and 2) valuable tool for reporting.

Timeframes

Typically, a one or two-year timeframe is sufficient for data retention. There was a client who went off its old system in February and, as the year rolled on, there were another two or three requests for historical reporting. From that point, demand was expected to diminish fairly quickly over the following years. In that particular case, much of the reporting was generated from the data warehouse, not necessarily from the system itself. HIPAA probably has the longest retention requirements, up to seven years. In situations like that, clients will shut down the system and keep everything intact (if they have space). Then, if needed, I/T would bring the system back up again to allow users to access the data for reporting. However, this is a rare situation. It isn't that common for users to have the need to go back to the old system five years after it was shut down.

Regulatory Requirements

When there is some kind of necessity from a regulatory standpoint, for example in the healthcare industry, organizations do need to retain historical data. Depending upon the nature of the industry, records may need to be retained for up to 10 years. So, there are some scenarios where, from a regulatory standpoint, organizations do need to keep their data and that's the scenario where we would look at a data warehouse. Otherwise, for most clients, the old system isn't just going to go away overnight when they begin using the new system. From an operational standpoint, it's still there. It's an archive at that point and, if the company's team members need to go back into it, they certainly can.

Platforms

When it comes to the regulatory side, FDA requirements to keep data for pharmaceutical companies or food and beverage manufacturers are for 10 years. This applies to record keeping on manufactured parts, as they must keep track of all the manufacturing of all the components used down to the raw material level, with traceability for all those items. Again, most clients don't operate in a stringent regulatory environment, so they don't have the need to hang on to the historical data archive as much. However, when they do, the data warehouse absolutely makes sense for them.

In some cases, it makes sense to keep the old system running for a period of time, maybe 1 or 2 years, where it's operational and available all the time. After that point, the utilization of that system typically diminishes quickly. One exception to that would be if the underlying platform is very old. We've migrated some clients from a UNIX platform onto something that was more current (i.e., a Windows platform), usually running a different ERP package. What happens to the old system? It's a little tough to keep a UNIX system running for very long especially if the hardware is somewhat old. In situations where that system was migrated to a Windows platform and then migrated off to another ERP application, it's not quite as difficult because clients can typically operate the Windows platform for quite a long time. In the migration process, we usually end up getting some number of data files off the old system to do the migration to the new system. But oftentimes, it's not the full set of data that should be looked at. Some data that should be included are master data and open transactions, like open sales, purchase orders, and production orders. However, the historical information about the sales orders, purchase orders, and production orders are typically not carried across to the new system.

They usually end up in the legacy system or in the data warehouse for future review.

Older Methodologies

Older methodologies include reel-to-reel tapes and more recently jukeboxes of tape cartridges for backup. One of the problems with these storage methodologies is that in order to be able to use those tapes, clients must have a system that is roughly the same as the equipment that created them. Sometimes, it's not so easy to reproduce that system even if you have those tapes.

That creates a different set of challenges. On the other side of that, some clients who had all of those records, at least with respect to any manufacturing records being kept on paper, would have to archive 10 years' worth of paper documents. The physical storage requirements for that alone were onerous. So, the move to electronic documentation can ultimately save a lot of time, money, and effort.

Chapter Summary

In Chapter 7, we reviewed ways to manage the data in the old system. Keeping the old system operational and loading data from the old system into a data warehouse are common solutions. One key consideration is the platform the old system is running on. Maintaining a current platform (e.g., Windows / SQL) is much simpler than maintaining something older (e.g., UNIX / BISAM).

CHAPTER 8 - CUSTOM SOFTWARE DEVELOPMENT

Under what conditions should an organization pursue custom software development?

While custom software development helps to fit the ERP application to existing business processes, there are cost / benefit tradeoffs to consider.

Custom software development can be a valuable tool in getting your ERP system into place. It helps to make your software fit better with the organization's business processes. The primary downside is that the custom software enhancements need to be reviewed and, in some cases, redone when the underlying software is upgraded to the most recent version. A potentially worse outcome is that custom software development is used to streamline an inefficient business process. In such cases, the process should be re-engineered before developing requirements for software development. In the discussion that follows, we'll discuss a few of the tradeoffs.

The 80 / 20 Rule

The 80 / 20 rule applies to ERP system implementations. Organizations should aim to get 80% of the functionality that it needs “out of the box”. In other words, get 80% of the required functionality without making any system modifications. For some of our clients, 80% was really all they needed. However, in some cases, there are unique challenges or specialized requirements within the organization. So, it becomes necessary to look for and select an out-of-the-box software package. The implementation team would typically aim to fulfill about 80% of the requirements with an out-of-the-box solution. The team would then look at what to customize and keep that fairly limited (tight in scope) to address the remaining 20% of the equation. The goal is to meet the specific needs of the organization; however, it has to be with respect to the way that the business processes should be run (rather than how they exist). One of the challenges that arises related to custom software development is when the client wants the consultants to customize the new solution to effectively work the same way the old solution did. This is definitely a difficult situation from a consultant standpoint, because in most cases, ERP systems are designed to follow the industry’s best practices.

Specialized Business Processes

If the consultants deviate from the way the new system is designed to function, there must be a good reason for it.

Generally, "It's because that's the way the old system worked." isn't a good enough reason for such a deviation.

It would require changing the business process in those cases and that's the change management side of implementing the new system. That can be one of the most difficult challenges with respect to implementation and acceptance of new technology.

In the late 1990's and early 2000's, the ERP systems were not always been a good fit for the client. Hence, custom software development was required to put some subsystems into place. These were often specific to the client's organization. As time has passed, the requirements for custom software development have diminished, partly because there are additional pieces of functionality in the software that fit business processes better. So, the software development requirement today is somewhat smaller than it was back then.

Third-Party Applications

The other thing that exists in the marketplace today, for virtually all major ERP solutions, is that most of them have an ecosystem of third-party applications built around them. These augment the core functionality of those systems. There are third-party packages that meet specific, unique industry needs like credit card processing, equipment rental, barcode scanning, or Electronic Data Interchange (EDI). There are quite a few products that tie into many of these mid-market ERP solutions. These applications meet a specific need that the publisher of the software may not have included in the core functionality of its product. These products are pre-integrated into the environment and do not require the custom development that used to be necessary in the past. Now, it is more a function of finding the correct third-party solution. This alleviates a lot of challenges related to ERP software upgrades because there is now a third-party software publisher who is managing that product. In other words, the third-party application provider is taking care of the updates and upgrades to the product.

Third-party application providers are maintaining their integration to the main ERP software publisher whether it's SAP, Oracle, Microsoft, NetSuite, or Intuit. The bottom line is they're managing that part of it, so the customer isn't hamstrung by the cost of rebuilding customizations when upgrading to a new version.

Even within the Microsoft ecosystem, this used to be one of the major knocks against products like Microsoft Dynamics

GP, NAV, and AX. Microsoft has spent a lot of time and effort over the past few years to make those upgrades more seamless for customers. Now, there is Dynamics 365 for Finance and Operations, formerly Dynamics AX, a completely SaaS, cloud-based solution.

Dynamics 365 can still be customized as there is a customization layer built into it. So, what we see today is the evolution of the software from the publisher side such that, where there is a case for customization, customers can easily upgrade to the latest versions. This is because there are long-term benefits for the software publishers to keep their customers on the latest and greatest version.

When customers fall off that cliff of having a customized solution, what often happens is that those customers choose not to do the upgrades. Further, at some point in time, they may choose not to continue to pay the annual software support and maintenance fees. That's a loss for the software publishers and they have considered ways to eliminate that loss. Even in a best-case scenario, for some organizations, there will always be a need for some element of customization.

Custom Software Development, Parameters, And APIs

The underlying structure of ERP software has evolved in recent years. In years past, consultants worked directly with the application's source code. Sometimes, they ended up taking a version of source code that was provided by the publisher, made some changes to it, and deployed new versions of the software. From an upgrade perspective, those situations were probably the most difficult for customers.

As time passed, parameters began to creep into ERP software. A parameter is a "switch" that changes the operation of software. In other words, different functionality is available in the system depending upon the setting of the parameter. Rather than going through the process of making modifications to the software, it just became a matter of setting parameters. SAP, Oracle, and Microsoft Dynamics have this functionality. As a result, operating the software became a little more complex often to the point where customers needed to have experts come in as consultants to set those parameters correctly.

One more observable change in this process is the concept of business objects or Application Program Interfaces (APIs). This occurs in SYSPRO and other applications.

SYSPRO does not allow changes to the base functionality of the software. Therefore, the base software always operates in the way its developers designed it. Basically, what third party providers and custom software developers do is write software that communicates to those business objects or APIs. In turn, the business objects will follow well-defined rules to create transactions within the system (e.g., add a sales order, receive cash against accounts receivable, issue a purchase order, etc.) Since those rules are always followed, the data is always consistent within the database.

Custom Software Development and Upgrades

One of the things that poses difficulties for the maintenance of the ERP system is the software upgrade process. As clients upgrade from version to version of the main publisher's software, the custom software development that was done along the way becomes a hindrance. This is because all those customizations must be carried forward into the new version. This effectively increases the cost of the upgrade. In most cases, carrying the upgrades forward is justified and cost-effective for the organization. In other cases, it would be more cost-effective for clients to follow the system's base functionality. This alleviates the need to carry forward the custom software development to subsequent versions.

Chapter Summary

In Chapter 8, we reviewed the pros and cons of custom software development. The 80 / 20 rule applies in that 80% of the functionality needed should be the standard software. Leveraging third-party applications and built-in APIs are generally preferable to developing custom software. Automating sub-optimal business processes with custom software development should only be undertaken as a last resort.

CHAPTER 9 - USER ADOPTION OF THE NEW ERP SYSTEM

What factors most influence user adoption of a new ERP system?

User adoption is an often overlooked but key ingredient in ERP systems implementations. I/T and Accounting support and smooth transfer of knowledge to the end-users are key factors.

Have you ever experienced or observed situations where a new system implementation was stymied because the users were unable or worse, unwilling, to use the new system? This issue seems to be more common in large organizations where systems functions are defined with some granularity. In the following discussion, we'll present some ideas that may be applicable to your situation.

I/T Support Alone is not Sufficient

If people are on board with the new system coming in and they're excited about it, then user adoption becomes much easier. However, if

1. Users are antagonistic to changing and bringing in new software,

2. Team members don't feel like management is engaged in the project,
3. This is a scenario where one executive decided to get the new software package,
4. The implementation of that new solution is largely being driven by I/T alone,
5. The CEO, the CFO, and other top management staff are not driving the project,

then the implementation becomes more challenging because I/T can't drive the project effectively by itself.

I/T needs buy-in from other parts of the organization, depending upon the nature of the organization. If it's a manufacturing organization, then Manufacturing certainly needs to be involved. Finance needs to be involved. The Supply Chain and Operation sides of the company need to be involved. Yes, even the Sales team needs to be involved. If these functional areas are going to need information from the system or work with internal information in the way of sales history, purchase orders, and inventory transactions in the system, then they must buy-in early in the process. If they don't, then the organization is going to have people who feel that their needs aren't being met and they're not being listened to in the process. Clearly, that's an internal issue more than a consultant's issue, however, it ends up falling, more often than not, on the consultants' shoulders. At the end of the day, the consulting team is tasked with getting the system online and making it work throughout the organization.

Training and Documentation

Another important factor is the investment in training. Organizations need to make an adequate investment and training and not try to "cheap out" in this area. While money is the lifeblood of the organization, ERP is the heart and brains. The ERP system in a business is arguably either the heart or the brain. Either way it's a pretty important organ because the ERP system is keeping the money flowing through the organization regardless of what type of business it is. The system is also handling all of the financial management for the organization. If we subscribe to the adage that money is the lifeblood of a business, then the ERP system is what's driving circulation. When we're looking at something that is this important to the organization in terms of data-driven decision-making and managing the finances of the organization, it is counterintuitive that some organizations try to skimp in places. One of the places that companies often skimp is either in training or documentation. The documentation is often directly tied to training because, in many cases, the documentation users are looking at and putting together is training-related. Further, the documentation becomes a post go-live resource for organization, so that executives won't have to call the consultants back in because somebody forgot how to perform some function in the system.

Change Management

Change management is how you prepare, equip and support team members to successfully adopt change. This is especially important in ERP systems implementations. There are actions you can take to influence users and encourage their adoption of the new ERP solution.

At an individual level, change management requires an understanding of how your team will experience and use the new ERP system and what tools they will need in the process. It also requires knowing what will help users make the implementation successful. It may useful to answer these questions:

1. What do users need to hear about the ERP system including why it's important to the organization?

2. When is the optimal time to train users about how they will be leveraging the new system?
3. How will SMEs coach team members in their respective functional areas to use the new system and, if needed, adjust their business processes?
4. What will make the ERP systems training and documentation and business process changes "stick" in team members' work?

Implementing a new ERP application will require organizational change management in conjunction with change at the individual level. At its core, it requires identifying the groups of people who will need to adopt the new ERP solution and in what ways they will need to work differently together to make the project successful. Organizational change management requires creating a customized plan to ensure key personnel receive the relevant communication, leadership, coaching, and training they need to make the implementation successful. Encouraging successful individual transitions will facilitate success at the organizational level.

In your ERP systems implementation, organizational change management will be needed in conjunction with project management (you will need both). Project management ensures that your ERP solution is designed, configured, and deployed correctly, while change management ensures the new system is effectively embraced, adopted, and, most importantly, used.

Transfer of Knowledge to the End-Users

There is often a need (and it is not always fulfilled) for the users to have some broad knowledge of how the system works as a whole. The policy and procedure documents help to accomplish that. At the most detailed level, there should be a set of desk procedures for team members to follow and as they go through the system. They would know exactly what screens they are supposed to go to and what kind of data and in which form should be populated on the fields. That will go a long way to help provide user adoption.

As mentioned earlier, getting the new system to work exactly like the old one may not be the best course of action, especially if resources (time and money) are limited. However, some customization may be warranted if the system changes can be completed quickly. For example, it may be helpful to make cosmetic changes to field names to be similar to what was in the old system, even though they have different functionality in the new system. So, if a few things occur like that where there are some similarities between the old and new systems, users will adapt more easily to the new package. During the implementation process, there also should be clear division of labor between the consultants and the users in the organization. We have seen cases where the consultants were very good at going through the process of getting everything running. They were running all the tests, defining all the processes, and making sure that everything flowed properly. Then, at the conclusion of the project, or near the conclusion of the project, the consulting team is withdrawn, leaving the system to the users. Unfortunately, when it came to the new system, the users were essentially lost. Without the consultants' help, the users did not have enough knowledge, skills, and tools to operate the new system successfully.

Involve Finance and Accounting Throughout the Implementation

It is important to get the Finance and Accounting teams involved early in the implementation process. In many cases, the Finance and Accounting teams don't get involved until late in the system implementation. So, all the operational aspects of the systems are working properly but there wasn't enough thought given to their impacts on the

G/L. As transactions flow correctly for shipping, receiving, and processing production orders, all of those transactions end up in the general ledger. Frequently (unfortunately) the G/L mappings that are set up during pilot testing aren't correct. It takes some time to unravel how system transactions were booked to the general ledger and correct the mappings.

Excel Spreadsheets

There was once a client for whom who the consulting team was implementing a new ERP software package. The client had been using an old ACCPAC system for its general ledger. However, Accounting had been tracking all of its costing and manufacturing operations in a series of Excel spreadsheets. The consultants went through the implementation of the new system and as they were getting into the standard cost of the product that the company manufactured, the client provided the formula it used for its product costing. This formula was entered and tested in the new system.

When it got to the point of validating the system, consultants were going through user acceptance testing. They started putting some transactions into the system and at that point reporting started to come out in the back end.

The client got very upset and said that the settings were wrong and the numbers that were being reported were incorrect. The consulting team went back to the system and determined that they had configured the system in a manner consistent with the formulas that the client had provided earlier. They went back to the client and said, "This is what you gave us and this is what we've entered in the system. When we put the transactions through, this is what we get."

What happened was that the Accounting team had to go back to the product costing spreadsheet and discovered that somebody had changed the formula in the Excel spreadsheet years prior. The subsequent spreadsheets were incorrect and ultimately it became something of a financial disaster for the organization. The Finance team realized this error had added millions of dollars to the bottom line for the product. The client ended up having to go in and, because it was a division of a much larger organization, restate its earnings. Ultimately, the CFO was fired and a couple of other people lost their jobs along the way. It turned out that the consultants and the new system were calculating product costs correctly. The cost numbers generated by the new system were correct, however, the old system had been wrong for years and had been causing incorrect earning statements to be generated for the organization. It was a disaster. Fortunately, the client moved forward, the new system was put in place, and, in the process, the management team learned the hard way the risks associated with managing the financial affairs of the company with an unsecured Excel spreadsheet. There's a good justification to get on to an ERP application if the organization has been running much of their business on Excel spreadsheets. With spreadsheets, the risk of having errors, a formula error for example, is very high. There have also been cases where Accounting personnel could not get the spreadsheet to reconcile. Rather than identify the discrepancy, they actually "plugged" the total with the number that tied out to everything else.

Chapter Summary

In Chapter 9, we covered user adoption of the new ERP system. In general, I/T cannot complete the implementation on its own. It takes a village. Training, documentation, and transfer of knowledge are key activities that increase user adoption. Finance should be involved at the beginning of the implementation rather than the end to ensure that sales, purchasing, inventory control, and production transactions impact the G/L correctly.

CHAPTER 10 - COMMON POST-IMPLEMENTATION ISSUES

After an ERP systems implementation has been completed, what issues should clients be mindful of?

For a period of time, immediately after an ERP systems implementation, it pays to be watchful. Identifying and resolving issues sooner will often be less expensive and time-consuming than doing so later.

Issue 1: Underestimating the scope of the overall project

If you think the system implementation is going to be finished at "go live", you're in for a surprise. In general, after a system goes live, there is often work planned for in the subsequent phases of the project and, unfortunately, work not planned for at all. As in many things, it is difficult to predict and address every scenario in which something might go wrong. The first few weeks after the ERP system goes live are the most critical.

What you need to be mindful of is that going through "go live" doesn't mean that's the end of the consultants' engagement with the system or with the organization. There's always some level of post "go live" support needed. In many cases, what we're talking about here is a continuous change element. The initial work up to going live is usually considered to be Phase 1. However, there could potentially be Phases 2, 3, 4, etc. which could be ongoing within organization. There are, in many cases, scenarios where the implementation of the new system is just the start of bringing in other elements to help the organization to be more efficient. For example, implementing bar code scanning, EDI, labor tracking, or Point of Sale (POS) modules may not within the scope of Phase 1. However, now that your organization has gotten through the initial implementation (e.g., the core financial functionality) of the new system, your team can look at secondary and tertiary elements of the overall implementation.

Issue 2: Not Preparing for Continuous Change Management

For some clients, the implementation creates a cycle that never ends or certainly doesn't end for years to come, depending upon where they are and where they are trying to go. Change management requires that organizations design a controlled process to identify and implement necessary changes to how work is performed with related adjustments to the ERP application. Clients who use a low-end accounting system with only core accounting functions often manage everything else in spreadsheets. If these clients have visions of going from this basic environment to the light-speed world of operating like Amazon.com, where everything is digital, they should be cautious and realize that it's not realistic to accomplish this kind of transformation in Phase 1. First, the timeframe for overall implementation will be significant. Second, the change management effort will place a strain on the organization. And third, the cost is going to be significant as well. It is important for the consulting team to be realistic with the client.

Clients should expect a multi-phased implementation process that ultimately allows them to accomplish their implementation objectives. However, that may take a year, two years, or three years, depending upon the organization and the requirements it must address. But that's not necessarily a bad thing. It allows executives to budget and manage costs over a multi-year timeframe, and from a financial standpoint, it allows the organization to spread those costs over multiple fiscal years so that the organization can absorb them over time as well.

Issue 3: Underestimating the Cost of the Overall Project

The other thing to look at is the support side of using the system. How well the users embrace the training in the beginning of the project will determine what the cost of the work on the backend of the implementation is going to be. For example, if during the initial training, people are sitting around, playing with their phones, and coming in and out of the training sessions and not embracing that training opportunity, then when the system goes live, there are going to be challenges. And after going live, there are going to be even more challenges. For example, if the finance team members weren't paying attention, and this is the first time they're going to do a month-end closing on their own on the live system, issues will most likely arise. The consulting team usually goes through the first month-end close with the accounting team. Now, it's the second time that they must go through month-end closing and they don't remember how to do it. The consulting team is going to have to help them and hold their hand through that process and that's an extra cost to the organization.

Issue 4: Insufficient Pilot Testing

The adage, "An ounce of prevention is worth a pound of cure" applies. In other words, a little precaution is preferable to a lot of fixing afterward. One issue that falls into the prevention category is pilot testing. The consultant team should coordinate at least two conference room pilot tests. The basic idea of the first pilot test is to work with some data that was manually keyed in. The objective of the second pilot test is to do some work with some data that has been migrated from the previous application.

In that second pilot test, in theory, users should be able see all the issues that are going to pop up after going live. It's a critical point in the process of implementation. If users let these issues slip all the way through and the system goes live, the things they didn't catch in that second pilot test are going to be compounded (in spades) when the system goes into production.

One case in point is the data migration. Data migration ideally should be pristine, so that the new system has the data from the old system and users can work with it going forward. In one client's situation, the data migration was not up to par. The data looked reasonable visually when users reviewed the screens, but processing transactions was a different story. For example, the data migration included open sales orders. Customer Service and Inventory Control had so much difficulty processing open sales orders that they couldn't get product shipped out the door. They had trouble getting shipping paperwork printed, generating invoices, and collecting cash. In this situation, not only was it a headache from a change management perspective, it became a serious financial problem as well. Before going live, it is very important to have as many of these issues as possible squared away during pilot testing.

Issue 5: Not Defining a Fallback Position

One of the issues that organizations should also be mindful of is not having a position to fallback to. If, for some reason, the organization goes live on a new application and there's a total meltdown on the new system, there must be a way to be able to fall back to a working position. Generally, this means going back onto the old system. It is not always advisable to use double entry to run parallel on both systems for a period of time because that process is extraordinarily expensive. Users are having a hard enough time dealing with the work that they have on a day-to-day basis. Keeping two ERP systems running at the same time in parallel is a very daunting task. In situations where there is no parallel run before cutting over, there needs to be a fallback position, which is typically to get back onto the old system if things go terribly out of control on the new one.

Issue 6: Not Learning From Earlier Phases to Make the Subsequent Phases Easier

In general, where there is an opportunity to take some small steps, there's a benefit of being able to learn from the earlier phases of the implementation. That way, the second and third phases can be executed more appropriately. When organizations try to take on Phase 1 through 3 at one time, they almost always end up having some difficulties that they could otherwise have avoided. For example, if an organization were to implement just the financial and logistics portions of the ERP system in Phase 1, then implementing the manufacturing aspects of the system can be approached in a more streamlined manner. In this scenario, the manufacturing module can be configured to meet the accounting requirements, which have already been well-defined.

Issue 7: Not Getting a Fast ROI from the Early Phases

Another reason why a multi-phase approach is recommended is that part of what your consulting team is trying to do for the organization is to get a relatively rapid return on the investment the organization has made in the new solution. If the implementation of the new system is going to take a year, then that means it's going to be a year before it can even begin to recapture any of the investment in the new system. However, if it's possible to implement a subset of the functionality that the executives ultimately want to have in Phase 1, then the organization can get a return on that investment fairly quickly. If Phase 1 can be completed in 90 days instead of a year, everybody is better off. The ownership and leadership of the organization would feel better at that point, because they've invested tens of thousands of dollars and see that they are getting a return on that investment. There's a confidence factor that goes up exponentially when the multi-phased approach is taken. This is a stark contrast to the, "I have to have everything, it all has to be done perfectly, and it all has to be done now." approach.

The latter scenario nearly always results in some horrifically bad projects where things really go awry. We caution clients to steer away from that as often as they can, because, at the end of the day, it's just not a good scenario for the consulting team or the client. The finger pointing that occurs, when the implementation takes too long or goes over budget, makes it a bad place for everybody. When the team goes through an implementation like this, these issues have to be discussed and resolved in pilot testing sessions and status meetings. It must be a team approach rather than "you versus me". It's "we" and that's how it is supposed to be. Everybody must work together to be successful. The consulting organization wants its clients to be happy with the outcome of the project.

Clients need to be better off, from a financial perspective, with the services of the consulting firm than without. If that doesn't happen, then both teams should be looking for another solution. The same can be said about the ERP system. In the early phases of deciding or in system selection phase, there's a need to determine what the benefit would be of having the ERP application versus the cost of not having it. From there, the executive team can do some analysis to calculate ROI, Net Present Value (NPV), Internal Rate of Return (IRR), or whatever makes the most sense for that organization. Once the implementation is done and a period of time goes by (e.g., 6 months), there is a need to take a look at what transpired after the ERP application went live. It's important to know how well it worked and ascertain if your organization is going to end up with the expected ROI.

Issue 8: Not Measuring Overall ROI

The fantasy dream world, from a consulting standpoint, is that the organization estimated the ROI of the project even before starting the implementation of the new system. Also, it would be ideal if the executive team had established some goals for what the new solution was going to do for the organization. Then it would be a straightforward process to compare the original estimates of ROI to the calculations for 6 months to a year after going live. Unfortunately, there have been a few clients that don't do that type of analysis. Further, they don't review their own internal business process analysis making it difficult for them to do any kind of real estimate of ROI after the fact. Without this data gathering and analysis, it is difficult to get a sense of the big picture. Your executive team should be able to determine whether or not the overall project was profitable and to what extent.

Chapter Summary

In Chapter 10, we covered common post-implementation issues. Underestimating scope, cost, and timing are the most common. One of the subtler issues is implementing phases that are too large. Taking an agile approach and implementing smaller phases allows clients to get a faster ROI as phases are implemented within the organization.

CHAPTER 11 - IoT AND ENTERPRISE RESOURCE PLANNING

What is IoT and how does it apply to enterprise resource planning?

The Internet of Things (IoT) refers to the connection of computer devices embedded in everyday objects. IoT has made its way into manufacturing processes to streamline and make them more efficient.

IoT refers to the web-enablement of traditional devices. Increasingly, we see the opportunities for connected devices that were, in the past, stand-alone. To illustrate, a vending machine, typically a stand-alone device, can be equipped with sensors and connected to the Internet. The vending machine can then transmit information about the items sold so that the vending machine operator knows when to come by and refill. The key benefit in this instance is that operator's route can be adjusted to skip the machines that still have sufficient inventory. Using a little math, the vending machine could signal when an item is about to sell out before it actually does!

Home automation is a big deal right now. Sensors installed within the home, can transmit information about temperature, humidity, sound, and how movement takes place inside the structure. One of the most common examples is the Nest thermostats that we're now seeing available on the market today that can be controlled by a smartphone or other mobile device.

Other examples include things we see every day and the adoption of IoT is growing exponentially. Things like the biometric devices that people are carrying and wearing are mobile-enabled, connected to the Internet via wireless networks, and transmitting useful information to their users.

One of the most common commercial implementations is in lighting and climate control in office buildings. The lights themselves are equipped with sensors that can sense temperature, humidity, and movement and transmit this data to lighting and HVAC control systems. The result is a significant saving in the cost of electricity.

There are a lot of benefits that come with IoT but a lot of challenges as well. Data security is the most pressing concern, however, that's a whole other area of the information technology world today.

In manufacturing and other industries, sensing the location and status of inventory, equipment, and personnel may be useful to make organizations more efficient.

Applications in Manufacturing

In manufacturing organizations, there is often equipment on the floor that the ERP application typically doesn't track. For example, the time spent on a particular operation in a production order is recorded, but the number of cycles a machine has been through is not. It is common to see equipment on the factory floor has been enabled with sensors and transmission devices, so that data about its operation can be communicated to a central location. Some of those pieces of equipment have a long mean time between failures and can notify maintenance personnel that a power supply or a circuit board should be replaced. The sensors can also communicate that a piece of physical machinery is always in use during the manufacturing process. The key advantage in this situation is that preventative maintenance can be scheduled at a convenient time rather than when a failure actually occurs. Also, the need for scheduled periodic maintenance can be reduced in favor of "as needed" predictive maintenance.

Some clients have large pieces of equipment that are deployed to customer locations in the field. Examples include manufacturers of machines used for packaging or bottle and can inspection. These machines are almost always complex pieces of equipment or equipment with many components. These pieces of equipment can be equipped with sensors that transmit how they are operating and can communicate to service personnel at the manufacturer or its customer's site that a component has failed or is about to fail. This affords the opportunity to replace the component before it goes out, which reduces or eliminates the downtime that might occur otherwise.

There are also opportunities where clients are producing pieces of equipment that move around. A case in point would be a vehicle manufacturer. The client's customer needs to know something about the pieces of equipment that are on the road, how the equipment is being maintained, and when the next service is required.

Finally, there's an opportunity to implement IoT in organizations whose business is measuring things. One example is a "clean room" facility that cleans and measures the residue that remains on a piece of equipment or component that's going into an aircraft. In those situations, those measuring devices also have the ability to transmit what they're measuring and eliminate a significant portion of manual data entry. This also eliminates the error that takes place in the recording of that data.

Product Testing

Predictive maintenance is probably the most obvious opportunity for IoT in manufacturing today, as there is often an immediate financial benefit for organizations that embrace it. We see this as an area in which there will be growth and expansion. Customers today also have higher demands of consultants and of their suppliers. One client provides heat testing and treatment services for the aerospace industry. One of the things that its customers, large aerospace companies, wanted from them was real-time data about the performance or the status of its customers' components. These components were pieces of equipment that were going into giant furnaces. To paint the picture, imagine a very large production facility with huge warehouse-sized furnaces. Literally, a small aircraft would fit into some of these furnaces. Then they would heat-treat the components by subjecting them to temperatures over one thousand degrees and then perform other operations on top of that. The client's customers were looking for the client to be able to give them real-time status reports. For example, “Where are my parts in your production process?” They were also looking for the ability for the furnaces to be web-enabled to the point where they could say, "Okay, Mr. Customer, your parts are in furnace number 127 and they're currently at 812 degrees. Oh, now they're at 813 degrees, and still within tolerance." The furnaces had to be web-enabled in order for the client to provide the real-time information its customers were looking for. For a period of time, this represented a competitive advantage for the client.

Record-Keeping for ISO Compliance

We’ve seen several instances where aerospace companies are very stringent about record keeping, especially if there's an ISO 9001 or some other compliance requirement for quality. Those situations require very good record-keeping about how the testing process went or how that heat treatment process described earlier was executed. Those records had to be kept on file for a lengthy period of time, which spanned many years.

In the aerospace industry, the general contractors, like Boeing and Lockheed Martin, were responsible for that record-keeping. Today, much of that has been pushed down to the subcontractors and they're the ones who have to do all of that record-keeping and tracking. That has become a major challenge for those smaller organizations.

Chapter Summary

In Chapter 11, we reviewed IoT and how it applies to ERP. With sensors and data analytics, systems can predict when equipment is about to fail. This provides maintenance personnel the opportunity to replace a failing component and minimize downtime. Real-time location tracking can be employed to monitor the location of assets in motion within and outside the manufacturing facility.

CHAPTER 12 - ARTIFICIAL INTELLIGENCE AND ENTERPRISE RESOURCE PLANNING

What is artificial intelligence and how might it apply to enterprise resource planning?

Artificial intelligence, in simplistic terms, is using computer systems to complete tasks that people would normally do. At minimum, artificial intelligence promises to support decision-making and automate certain supply chain functions.

In combination with IoT functionality, artificial intelligence (AI) could well become the "brain" that controls entire manufacturing plants. There is still much work to be done in this area, however, the rate of progress is accelerating. In other words, ten years ago, what took ten years to accomplish, will only take a few years today. This will be an exciting area to watch as innovations are brought to market.

Artificial Intelligence and Big Data

Big data refers to extremely large data sets that can be analyzed by computer systems to reveal patterns or trends. IoT is, for better or for worse, a source of lots and lots of data that can then lead us to questions about big data. Business intelligence tools like Watson Analytics, Microsoft Power BI, and Tableau Desktop can serve to harness these mountains of data. Once the business analytics are in place, the next step in the process is to interpret the data that's coming out of these IoT devices. An increasingly important question is, "How can artificial intelligence be applied to enterprise resource planning?" There are many different opportunities to leverage artificial intelligence within your organization, including those that apply to supply chain, inventory control, production, and ordering processes. For example, today, buyers and planners are responsible for keeping inventory at optimal levels. Sales forecasting, Master Production Scheduling (MPS), and Materials Requirements Planning (MRP) guide many organizations' materials management. At some time in the not so distant future, these roles will be replaced by intelligent systems that can keep track of inventory values, determine when inventory will be depleted, and order replacement parts. These parts will arrive just in time to be pulled from their location by a robot or automated conveyor system for the next production order. The next evolution of this paradigm shift is when one organization's

AI communicates with other organization's AIs to keep their respective supply chains running smoothly.

Natural Language Processing

We live in a world today where we can choose from Siri, Google Assistant, Alexa, or Cortana to gain access to an artificial intelligence platform. We can verbally ask for information, have an intelligent agent retrieve it and give it back to us verbally or visually. For example, someone on the shop floor can verbally request the drawings for the part he or she is working on at the time. IBM, Google, Amazon, and Facebook are expending tremendous amounts of human and financial resources in this area. It's going to be an interesting journey. Microsoft is certainly moving in this direction. Cortana Analytics integration is one of the newest features offered in its ERP solutions. We expect this trend to continue as new and more powerful computing platforms become available and new versions of software are released.

Balance Inventory Carrying Cost and Product Availability

Given a source of historical data, there are ways to predict what is likely to happen in the future. For example, it is possible to assess the risk of a forest fire occurring a certain area using historical temperature, humidity, rainfall patterns, and actual incidents of forest fires. If we extend that concept a little, we can see ways to make use of these predictive tools in enterprise resource planning. One requirement that has come up frequently in client organizations is the ability to forecast future demand for products. Today, it's more art than science.

We've observed that, in many situations, the forecast is optimistic based upon the Sales team's projections. Similarly, executives of the company might have an overly rosy view of what's going to happen in the future. The forecast then drives MRP to recommend purchasing more material than the Operations team actually needs. As a result, this increases inventory carrying costs. The other side of the issue is not having enough inventory. In these situations, shipments may be delayed due to being out of stock of key component materials. This in turn impacts cash flow and future sales. The forecasting methodology can be refined in such a way where it's optimized to minimize inventory carrying costs and the opportunity cost of lost sales due to "out of stock" situations. The forecast can be self-correcting and, if in error, can be adjusted based on actual demand. This will serve to reduce the production of finished goods and the ordering of component raw materials. The entire MRP shifts as the sales forecast is adjusted. Artificial intelligence can be inserted into the process so that sales forecasting is significantly more accurate. This creates a number of opportunities. For example, in addition to historical sales of products, macroeconomic, social media, and other publicly available data can be included in the forecasting algorithm. The resulting models can then generate even more accurate forecasts.

Here are some possible data elements that might be used to predict customer demand:

- Historical sales by month
- Trends year to year
- Seasonality
- Overall industry demand
- Social media chatter related to the product or product category
- Publicly available data (e.g., industry associations. government agencies, academic studies)

Augmented Reality

Another set of innovations has become popular in recent years. It can be called artificial intelligence to some extent but deserves their own classification. These are virtual reality, augmented reality, and mixed reality. Here's how to distinguish them:

Virtual reality (VR)	3 dimensional images Human interaction • Goggles or helmet with screen • Gloves with sensors
Augmented reality (AR)	View of the real world Superimposes computer generated images Composite view
Mixed reality (MR)	A form of augmented reality Somewhere between VR and AR View of the real world Superimposes virtual objects that also appear to be real

We encountered an interesting example of augmented reality in the construction industry. When constructing a building, having virtual access to the blueprints and data on what needs to be constructed can be very valuable. In this example, the developer was able to apply augmented reality to the construction of a commercial building. Construction workers, wearing headsets, were able to complete construction tasks with visual cues. They put framing, electrical, and plumbing components in the right places without having to refer to the blueprints. All necessary information was visually in front of them, available through augmented reality.

Augmented reality opens doors to other opportunities within business organizations. Imagine training employees in a manufacturing or production facility. With augmented reality, clients can do that in a virtual world and begin to elevate the skill sets of machine operators. Supervisors can show production personnel exactly what they need to be doing in an augmented view rather than taking time on (or off) the production floor for conventional training. There are a lot of opportunities in this area in manufacturing organizations and service organizations. Historically, teaching production personnel how to complete complex tasks has been a major endeavor. Being able to do that in a virtual world would enable manufacturing and services organizations to bring people up to speed quickly and conserve financial resources.

Headsets

Imagine having shop floor personnel with augmented reality readily available to them through headsets with audio, video, natural language processing, and speech synthesis. They will have all of the information necessary to assemble the parts and be able to transmit all of the production order information for the ERP application with one hands-free device. Web-enabled cameras can capture video and images of the production process to help identify errors. Built-in microphones and natural language processing can facilitate the process of data capture for the ERP application. Built-in speakers will provide the ability to quickly communicate with supervisors and co-workers. Conventional-looking eyeglasses or safety glasses will replace the bulky headsets available today.

Some of the technology we described in this chapter might sound like something from a science fiction movie. However, here we are today with these capabilities becoming part of everyday life. Some of the things that General Electric has already implemented in some of their heavy production are truly innovative. Many of these technologies are already being utilized at the Fortune 500 level. We expect that they will, within a relatively short time frame, trickle down to small and medium-sized businesses just like yours.

Chapter Summary

In Chapter 12, we reviewed artificial intelligence and how it applies to ERP. Business analytics and managing big data are basic requirements. Supply chain management and sales forecasting are key opportunities. Augmented reality, coupled with artificial intelligence, could significantly improve the financial metrics in manufacturing firms.

CHAPTER 13 – THE FUTURE OF ENTERPRISE RESOURCE PLANNING

What's next for enterprise resource planning?

Cloud computing, artificial intelligence, automated manufacturing, and losing jobs to automation are all hot topics of discussion. Let's take look at the future prospects for ERP applications.

Cloud Applications

We see the shift to cloud computing continuing to improve the cost-effectiveness of ERP applications. The cloud is the more sensible approach in the long-run. Many organizations have made large investments in server hardware and then utilized a relatively small fraction of its capabilities. Today, clients can effectively "rent" that functionality in a cloud model, sharing computing resources with other organizations. The result is that the physical hardware itself is getting a much higher level of utilization as virtual machines are provisioned on it. So, for the foreseeable future, the shift to the cloud will continue.

As of this writing, established manufacturing organizations seem to be hesitant to move their hardware and software off-premises or into the cloud. Many I/T executives have been resistant and prefer to keep everything on-premises, perhaps for control. In some exceptional cases, mostly large companies, I/T is very well-developed. These organizations have lots of personnel, large server rooms, good electrical power, fast Internet connections, air conditioning, and redundancy. From that standpoint, these firms can do many things on-premises. Smaller organizations generally cannot support that kind of infrastructure and are better candidates to pursue a cloud solution for their ERP applications as they will be able to quickly implement new features in the software.

The hybrid model for I/T infrastructure is becoming more common. In these cases, a portion is kept on-premises and a portion resides in the cloud. We see the initial steps to implement cloud backup and disaster recovery. Secondary functions might be migrated into the cloud, keeping the primary operation on-premises. As time goes on, more and more computing infrastructure and business applications functionality will get pushed into the cloud and, at some point, cloud computing will become the de facto standard.

Artificial Intelligence

We've covered some interesting technologies, including IoT, and that the connectedness of devices and software will provide executives with better and more timely information with which to make decisions. We see this trend continuing and growing exponentially, as organizations are presented with more and more information. We are already seeing that today, because businesses are generating and capturing data from various sources. That doesn't necessarily make it easier for humans to make decisions. This is one of the challenges and opportunities for artificial intelligence. At some point, we may find that the human brain just can't make sense of all of that data. However, a machine can. It can consolidate the information and present options with corresponding probabilities based on the data available.

Machines can do the heavy lifting, processing the data and painting a picture of what may be happening. Whether it is labor data collected on the shop floor, financial performance indicators, or data from the human resources information system, consolidation of these massive quantities of data will, at some point, become a major challenge for humans. We also foresee a shift to faster, smarter machines. It will be an evolution rather than an overnight occurrence. If Google can enable cars that drive themselves, imagine what can be accomplished using similar intelligence in a manufacturing environment.

Salesforce.com recently announced the introduction of Einstein, an artificial intelligence component of its well-known software as a service (SaaS) sales automation platform. We think that this will be more common as software applications get rolled out. These applications will simply end up having an AI component built into them. Sometime, in the not-so-distant future, there is going to be AI functionality built into ERP applications. The AI will help with the processing and interpretation of transactions and decision-making in manufacturing organizations. Imaging the notification and alert functions in your smart phone, but on a much, much larger scale.

We briefly touched on the opportunity to go and grab data from outside the organization. Historically, ERP applications have been focused on internal sales and purchase order processing, financial reporting, inventory control, and manufacturing. However, there are some interesting external sources of data that might be useful to merge into the ERP application, including IoT data mentioned earlier. Other types of external data include geographic, demographic, and psychographic, some of which might be useful in the ERP application.

Machines Manufacturing Machines

The term "lights out manufacturing" refers to situations in which a manufacturing facility can operate with little or no human presence. People are required for the preparation of component materials, receipt of finished goods, and quality assurance. Opportunities for hybrid scenarios exist in which one process or one shift could be "lights out". The term automatic factory applies to situations where there is little or no human intervention. For example, FANUC, a Japanese robotics manufacturer, uses robots to manufacture robots at a rate of about 50 per day. Not only are the lights turned off, but the heating and air conditioning as well. It seems like something out of science fiction, however, it's happening today in advanced manufacturing facilities. Machines making machines is a little bit unnerving, however, they are a long way from taking over the world.

Losing Jobs to Automation

One of the challenges is that the U.S. has lost more jobs to automation than to offshore competitors. If current trends continue, job losses will expand rapidly. So, what does the future hold? Many of the innovations we've talked about involve replacing people, which is good for business. Is there a point at which to strike a balance? If a machine can run 24 x 7 x 365 with low maintenance requirements and it can replace a human operator, why would an organization not automate assuming it was cost-effective? These are macroeconomic and geopolitical issues that are outside of our areas of expertise, however, we are already seeing it happening and beginning the search for answers.

CHAPTER 14 – AFTER ENTERPRISE RESOURCE PLANNING

What comes after Enterprise Resource Planning?

The future is bright for blending applications, artificial intelligence, blockchain, automated software development, and business process optimization.

Overview

The landscape is shifting for Enterprise Resource Planning and this movement can be observed as a blending of business applications. In the past, the ERP system was deployed as a stand-alone application. In addition, even today, Customer Relationship Management, Marketing Automation, and E-commerce Systems are sold and installed as stand-alone systems. In the "beginning", there were accounting systems and all they did was basic accounting. The bulk of the work these systems were designed to do was to manage the general ledger. Not long afterwards, functionality for accounts receivable and accounts payable were added.

It seems rudimentary today, but that was it, nothing more. These were merely basic stand-alone accounting systems.

To make matters more complicated, companies implemented separate stand-alone inventory systems and stand-alone manufacturing systems. One major drawback: All of these systems were separate from one another. Over time, these stand-alone systems were "pulled together" into what we now know of today as ERP, which supports the business functions across the entire business. ERP was the creation of an integrated platform that supported the work of functional areas that were peripheral to accounting system but related to it. It is through this process that we got to where we are today.

Blending, Integrating, Innovating

So, what comes next? In a word, "blending". This can be observed today in the innovations being made by the providers of business application software. For example, NetSuite's integrated platform that contains:

- Accounting
- Inventory control
- Manufacturing
- e-Commerce
- Marketing Automation
- Customer Relationship Management
- Business Intelligence

all of which are seamlessly integrated and available on a subscription basis.

Microsoft is doing similar things with its Dynamics 365 solution which includes ERP, CRM and well-developed analytics capabilities. All these are seamlessly blended together to form what is best described as a business application. Using this blended application model, you can purchase licenses or subscriptions for just the functionality you need. Of course, companies can obtain licenses for the entire suite, which all depends on the organization's requirements. It's important to understand that these business applications are available on a subscription basis. In essence, subscribers simply pay a per-user-per-month licensing fee plus implementation costs. No one has really come up with a term for this software model. For now, we'll just call it a unified business application. It seems clear that we are headed towards a world of unified business applications.

Simplification

Many will agree that ERP is complex especially when integrated with CRM and other business systems. Also, it has been said that simplicity is the ultimate level of sophistication. Then how can we make ERP simple? The users of the application are for whom the ERP system should be made simple. It seems as if nothing about ERP is simple. There are many technical reasons. First, ERP systems need to work for many types of businesses and most on the market today were for manufacturers, distributors, retail organizations, and professional service organizations. All of those industries are distinct and have different requirements and business challenges. In the future, systems will be designed to be configurable for any business. Another aspect of simplicity will be how AI can be used to simplify users' experience so that they are not overwhelmed with all of the options, transactions, data capture, and business processes. Some elements of usability are getting better, but major strides are yet to come. Those are the challenges for ERP software providers and for companies who are deploying an ERP solution. This will be especially challenging for companies that are still using legacy technology and clients who have not upgraded their ERP system in many years. Organizations that do not avail themselves of the opportunity to take advantage of that simplicity will yield competitive advantage to their competitors.

Common Data Model

Stand-alone applications each have their own databases. This increases the complexity and need for integration tools. To address this, the "Common Data Model" was developed. The Common Data Model approach is interesting as it affords a way to standardize and centralize the data structures of related software applications. This streamlines the process of integrating inventory control with both manufacturing and accounting. Taking this one step further, the database of the future will be amorphous in the sense that it may begin as a blank slate which will configure itself to into the structure that best supports the organization's business processes.

The Software Writes Itself

In parallel, the software will "write itself" piece by piece, adding components to the software as they are needed. When the database and software are in their final forms, the result will be a highly-customized business application. The notion that the software writes itself is appealing. Today, there are pre-canned systems from various publishers that have strengths and weaknesses. The challenge of implementation is to customize one of them to fit into the business processes, reengineered to support the organization's strategic plan. This is rarely a straightforward task. Having the software write itself to match the organization's current business process and then re-configure itself as needed afterwards is intriguing.

Blockchain Technology

Blockchain is not a new concept. It is simply technology that provides a secure mechanism for recording transactions. People are mostly familiar with the use of blockchain to account for and manage cryptocurrencies. However, this is just one application of the blockchain functionalities. Blockchain technology is being applied to supply chain management, the discipline of ensuring that materials used in the manufacturing process arrive in a timely, cost-effective manner. This will open the door to some very interesting innovation and ultimately impact various business applications including what we know today as ERP and CRM.

This blockchain / supply chain scenario creates the opportunity for vendors and customers to have very clear and traceable visibility of the transactions in the supply chain. For instance, it could begin with something as simple as recording purchase orders and sales orders. If we take that one step further, a sales order acknowledgement could be included in the blockchain. When the material is about to be shipped, the expected delivery date could be recorded in the blockchain. The blockchain can record that the parts have been received and passed inspection. Finally, the invoice and payment transactions can be recorded in the block chain.

EDI & Blockchain

As we think about the basic nature of Electronic Data Interchange (EDI) and blockchain today, there's almost a perfect one-to-one correspondence between how things work in EDI and how it could be structured using blockchain technology. One very appealing feature that, as transactions are recorded, visibility is essentially immediate. Another appealing feature is that with all parties up and down, the supply chain can have visibility of the transactions as they occur. Blockchain is designed to be an immutable record of a transaction with a complete audit trail. Since all parties agree that the transactions recorded in the blockchain accurately represent what actually transpired, this situation creates some interesting opportunities. One example in the healthcare industry is the creation and maintenance of medical records. Everything that relates to a patient's medical history could be stored in a blockchain structure. This is useful because it is not changeable. No one can forge the results of a lab test or a DNA test if it becomes an issue in a legal dispute or criminal proceeding. The record is immutable leaving little room to question how and when the transactions took place.

Artificial Intelligence & Enterprise Resource Planning

AI has filtered into a number of ERP applications and in sales force automation systems. As of this writing, AI seems to be focused on reporting, in terms of how to generate reporting based upon natural language inquiries. The more interesting question is what comes next for AI and ERP. One impact of having AI in ERP is that it will be able to tell us when things are taking place and when certain things need to be done. For example, when inventory levels are low, the system will provide advanced notifications like, "Based on the current level of production, the plant will run out of X component on Y date. In order to prevent this from happening, orders for Z units will be placed with the supplier now." One of the challenges that we see in ERP, and other systems, today is that there is an extraordinarily large amount of data being created. Because of this, it's quite difficult for people to get what they need in terms of reporting. If you look at ancillary technologies like IoT where we are adding more devices on a production line or into other areas of the business, you realize that the growth of data has been exponential. The challenge with growth is that more data doesn't necessarily make it easier for humans to get the information that they need. Instead, it often makes it harder. An intelligent system can filter through that data very quickly and extract relevant business insights and take action. More importantly, this can be done on a proactive rather than reactive basis. This is directionally where we see the integration of AI into business applications.

It seems as if every organization has a different methodology for sales forecasting. AI will become useful in the sales forecasting process, because it will take inputs that we wouldn't normally consider. Social media, for instance, can be used in situations where transactions are transmitted back and forth between business partners. These represent a plethora of data which AI could use to create models for sales forecasting. Today, systems interact with people. A few years from now these interactions will be between various intelligent systems.

Software Development

From a software development perspective, in order to make systems simple for the end-user, it requires significant effort in software development. This means that the business applications software providers must apply more effort to make it simple for the end-user. Steve Jobs and his team were able to accomplish this at Apple. In order for Apple products to be simple to use, a lot of work and ingenuity went into the design and the software development of the iMac, iPod, iTunes, iPhone, and iPad. These are the kinds of things that business application providers will need to do to make their products simple for customers.

Business Process Optimization

Business process optimization represents another opportunity. Today, we assist clients in analyzing and reengineering their business processes. The objective is to streamline operations and reduce wasted effort. Often, companies must change their businesses process to fit with the system. In situations where business processes are sub-optimal, we typically suggest changing it rather than automated it. In the future, intelligent business applications will be implemented using an organization's existing business processes. Here, the simplicity is that the implementation is simple. Once installed the business application will identify operational bottlenecks and reconfigure itself to address them. In parallel, it will enforce changes to business processes to fit the new system configuration. We believe that there is groundbreaking work to be done in this area.

Benefits & Opportunities

Today, it seems as if the major concern is about the information coming out of the ERP system. This is very relevant, however, if more focus is placed on the user experience and the system is simpler for the users to use and get the data into the system. There will be a number of benefits including:

- Significantly fewer errors
- Reduced implementation challenges
- Shorter time to user acceptance
- Faster ROI

This presents an opportunity for all business application software publishers, as anyone who has implemented an ERP solution knows that it is not an easy thing to do. ERP software providers must put more focus and effort into providing the functionality customers need while making the user experience simple.

###

We hope that this book has been helpful to you and that you've enjoyed reading it as much as we've enjoyed writing it. We are always happy to help others using what we've learned and would like to offer a way to continue our conversation.

As a thank you for purchasing our book, we are offering an introductory course on artificial intelligence titled, "Artificial Intelligence - How to prepare yourself for the era of AI". In this course, we will explain what artificial intelligence is, why it's important, how it's begin used, and how to prepare for primary and secondary roles in AI. This course, a $249.95 value, is provided to you at the discounted price of only $49.95.

To register, go to http://bit.ly/AIIntroCourse